AF725291

A Beginner's Guide to PHP

by LAEL A. ALEXANDER

Global Institute of Science & Technology

"Building Blocks" is an educational series that is guided by the practice of Dr. Lael A. Alexander in order to encourage elemental literacy in American Students.

Global Institute of Science and Technology
Tulsa, Oklahoma Published by Penguin & Rook LLC

A Beginner's Guide to

PHP

by LAEL A. ALEXANDER

Global Institute of Science & Technology

Book Title: Building Blocks
Subtitle (optional): A Beginner's Guide to *Php*
Author: Dr. Lael A. Alexander
Publisher Information: Penguin & Rook LLC
Edition: First Edition
Date of Publication: March 17, 2024

Copyright Page

- **ISBN:** TBD
- **Publisher Information:** Penguin & Rook LLC
- **Disclaimer:**
  The author and publisher have made every effort to ensure the accuracy of the information contained in this book. However, the book is provided "as is" without warranty of any kind, either expressed or implied. Readers are encouraged to seek professional advice for specific use cases.

Dedication

For those who dream of a decentralized future where technology empowers everyone equally.

Contents

Preface for PHP Book

For decades, PHP has been the backbone of web development, powering millions of websites and applications, including some of the most popular content management systems like WordPress. Its ease of use, flexibility, and robust community support have made it a reliable choice for developers of all skill levels.

This book takes you on a journey through PHP's evolution from a simple scripting language to a powerful tool for building dynamic, database-driven applications. Whether you're looking to build APIs, integrate PHP with modern front-end frameworks, or use PHP in blockchain systems, this book will provide you with the knowledge and confidence to do so.

Introduction for PHP Book

PHP is a server-side scripting language designed to create dynamic web pages and applications. In this book, you'll learn how to harness PHP's capabilities to interact with databases, create secure APIs, and build web applications that are efficient and scalable. Starting with the basics, this book gradually introduces advanced topics, including PHP frameworks like Laravel and integrating PHP with modern technologies.

The practical examples in this book are geared toward real-world applications, helping you not only learn the syntax and tools but also how to apply them effectively.

Notes from the Author on PHP

PHP may seem like a legacy tool to some, but its adaptability makes it a vital part of many modern tech stacks. I've used PHP to connect traditional web systems to blockchain and other innovative technologies. My goal with this book is to showcase how PHP can still shine in modern development, particularly for backend logic and data-driven systems.

Chapter 1: Introduction to PHP and Databases

Understanding PHP

PHP, which stands for Hypertext Preprocessor, is a widely-used open-source scripting language that is particularly suited for web development. It can be embedded in HTML, which allows for the creation of dynamic web pages that can interact with databases. Understanding PHP is essential for anyone looking to manage data on the web, as it provides the foundation for building applications that can dynamically generate content based on user input and interaction. As a beginner, grasping the fundamentals of PHP will enable you to create applications that are not only functional but also efficient and secure.

One of the key features of PHP is its ability to connect to various database systems, making it an essential tool for developers working with data-driven applications. MySQL is the most commonly used database with PHP, thanks to its robustness and ease of integration. By learning PHP, you will discover how to perform operations such as creating, reading, updating, and deleting records in a database, collectively referred to as CRUD operations. These operations are the backbone of most web applications, allowing users to interact with data seamlessly.

PHP's syntax is designed to be easy to learn, especially for those who may not have a background in programming. It closely resembles C, Java, and Perl, making it accessible to individuals transitioning from other professions or educational backgrounds. With its straightforward structure, new learners can quickly pick up essential concepts such as variables, arrays, loops, and functions. This simplicity is one reason why PHP remains a popular choice among beginners and seasoned developers alike.

In addition to its core functionality, PHP offers a range of frameworks and libraries that can enhance your development experience. Frameworks like Laravel and CodeIgniter provide pre-built modules and tools that streamline the development process, allowing you to focus on building unique features for your application. These frameworks also promote best practices in coding, which is crucial for maintaining clean and efficient code as your projects grow in complexity. Understanding how to leverage these tools can significantly accelerate your learning curve and improve your skill set.

As you delve deeper into PHP, you will also learn about security measures that are vital when working with databases. Learning how to sanitize inputs, manage sessions, and secure data against common vulnerabilities like SQL injection is crucial for building safe and reliable applications. This knowledge is especially important for career changers and students entering the tech industry, where understanding security best practices is a fundamental aspect of web development.

By mastering PHP and its database interactions, you will be well-equipped to tackle a range of projects and advance your career in the field of web development.

Importance of Databases in Web Development

Databases play a crucial role in web development, serving as the backbone for storing, managing, and retrieving data efficiently. In today's digital landscape, the ability to handle large volumes of data is essential for creating dynamic and interactive web applications. For career-changed professionals and students venturing into the world of PHP and databases, understanding the importance of databases is fundamental to the development process. Databases not only provide a structured way to manage data but also improve the overall performance and scalability of web applications.

One of the primary functions of a database in web development is to facilitate data storage. Websites often require the management of various types of information, such as user profiles, product listings, and transactional data. A relational database management system (RDBMS) allows developers to organize this information in tables, making it easier to access and manipulate when needed. For beginners in PHP, leveraging databases enables them to create applications that can handle user input and store data persistently, which is a significant step towards building functional web applications.

Moreover, databases enhance the efficiency of data retrieval operations. In a web application, users expect quick responses when they perform actions like searching for products or submitting forms. Databases are designed with indexing and querying capabilities that allow developers to optimize these operations. By using SQL (Structured Query Language), PHP developers can write complex queries to retrieve specific data quickly, thus improving user experience. This efficiency is particularly important for applications with a large user base or extensive datasets, where performance can significantly impact user satisfaction and engagement.

Another vital aspect of databases is their ability to maintain data integrity and security. In web development, ensuring that data remains accurate and protected from unauthorized access is paramount. Databases offer various features such as constraints, transactions, and user permissions that help maintain data integrity. For professionals transitioning into this field, understanding how to implement these features in PHP applications is critical. This knowledge not only helps in building secure applications but also fosters trust among users, who expect their data to be handled responsibly.

Finally, databases support the scalability of web applications. As businesses grow and their user bases expand, the need for applications to handle increased data loads becomes inevitable. A well-designed database can accommodate growth by allowing developers to scale their applications horizontally or vertically. For newcomers to PHP and databases, learning how to design scalable database architectures will empower them to create applications that can evolve over time. This adaptability is essential in a rapidly changing technology landscape, where user needs and market demands can shift unexpectedly. Understanding the importance of databases equips new developers with the skills necessary to build robust and responsive web applications.

Overview of PHP Database Interaction

PHP, or Hypertext Preprocessor, is a widely-used open-source scripting language that is especially suited for web development. One of its core strengths lies in its ability to interact seamlessly with various database systems. This interaction is crucial for dynamic web applications, where data storage, retrieval, and manipulation are essential for functionality. Understanding how PHP interacts with databases lays the foundation for building robust web applications that efficiently handle user data, session management, and content management.

At the heart of PHP's database interaction capabilities is the ability to connect to databases using extensions such as MySQLi and PDO (PHP Data Objects). MySQLi is specifically designed for MySQL databases and offers both procedural and object-oriented programming interfaces. PDO, on the other hand, is a more versatile option that supports multiple database systems, including MySQL, PostgreSQL, and SQLite. This flexibility allows developers to write code that can work with different database types, making PDO a preferred choice for many professionals looking to future-proof their applications.

Establishing a connection to a database is the first step in PHP database interaction. This process involves specifying the database server, username, password, and database name. Once connected, developers can execute SQL queries to perform a variety of operations, such as retrieving data, inserting new records, updating existing entries, or deleting data. PHP's simplicity in executing these SQL commands, combined with its error handling capabilities, makes it an accessible option for beginners who are new to database management.

Data retrieval in PHP typically involves using SELECT statements, which allow developers to fetch specific data from one or more tables. Once the data is retrieved, it can be displayed dynamically on web pages, enhancing the user experience. Additionally, PHP provides various functions to process and manipulate the fetched data, making it easier to format and present it according to the application's requirements. This capability is particularly beneficial for creating interactive features such as user profiles, blog posts, and product listings.

Security is a critical aspect of PHP database interaction, especially when handling user input. To protect against common vulnerabilities such as SQL injection, developers are encouraged to use prepared statements and parameterized queries. These techniques ensure that user inputs are treated as data rather than executable code, significantly improving application security. For new learners, understanding these best practices is essential not only for building functional applications but also for safeguarding sensitive data against potential threats.

Chapter 2: Setting Up Your Environment

Installing PHP

Installing PHP is an essential step for anyone looking to develop applications that utilize databases effectively. PHP, a widely-used server-side scripting language, is particularly popular for web development due to its ease of integration with various databases. The installation process can vary slightly depending on the operating system you are using, but there are general steps that will guide you through the process, ensuring you can start coding without delay.

For Windows users, the easiest way to install PHP is by using a package manager such as XAMPP or WAMP. These packages come bundled with PHP, Apache, and MySQL, providing a complete environment for web development. After downloading the installer from the official website, you simply need to run the setup and follow the prompts. Once installed, you can verify the installation by creating a simple PHP file that calls the phpinfo() function, which will display the PHP configuration details.

For macOS users, the installation process involves using Homebrew, a popular package manager. First, ensure that Homebrew is installed on your machine. You can then use the terminal to execute the command `brew install php`, which will download and install the latest version of PHP. Similar to the Windows setup, you can confirm the installation by creating a PHP file in the web server directory and accessing it via your browser. This will help you ensure that PHP is running correctly on your macOS environment.

Linux users typically install PHP using the terminal. The installation can vary depending on the distribution, but for Ubuntu, the command `sudo apt-get install php` will suffice. After installation, you may want to install additional modules depending on your project requirements, such as `php-mysql` for MySQL database integration. Like other operating systems, testing your installation with a simple PHP file will help you confirm that everything is set up correctly.

Once PHP is installed, configuring the environment is the next crucial step. This involves editing the `php.ini` file, where you can set various directives like error reporting and memory limits to suit your development needs. It is essential to review these settings, especially if you are working on database-driven applications, as they can significantly affect performance and debugging. Proper configuration will provide you with a robust foundation for developing PHP applications, making the learning process smoother and more efficient.

Choosing a Database Management System

Choosing a Database Management System (DBMS) is a critical decision for anyone looking to work with PHP and databases. A DBMS allows users to create, manage, and manipulate databases efficiently. When selecting a DBMS, several factors come into play, including the specific requirements of the application, scalability, performance, and ease of use. It's essential to understand the different types of database systems available, such as relational databases, NoSQL databases, and in-memory databases, as each serves different purposes and use cases.

Relational Database Management Systems (RDBMS) are the most common choice for PHP applications. These systems, such as MySQL, PostgreSQL, and SQLite, organize data into tables that can be easily related to one another through keys. RDBMSs use Structured Query Language (SQL) for data manipulation, making them a suitable choice for beginners familiarizing themselves with database operations. For those starting, MySQL is particularly popular due to its extensive community support, documentation, and integration capabilities with PHP, making it an ideal choice for new learners.

NoSQL databases, such as MongoDB and Cassandra, offer flexibility in data storage and retrieval, dealing well with unstructured or semi-structured data. These systems are designed to scale horizontally and can handle large volumes of data across distributed systems. While they may present a steeper learning curve for beginners, they are valuable for applications requiring quick data access and high performance. Understanding the specific needs of your application will help determine if a NoSQL database is more suitable than a traditional RDBMS.

Another important factor to consider is the community and support surrounding a DBMS. A robust community can provide valuable resources, tutorials, and forums for problem-solving. Beginners will benefit from choosing a DBMS with a strong user base and comprehensive documentation. This support network can serve as a lifeline when encountering challenges, particularly when integrating the database with PHP. Additionally, evaluating the availability of tools and libraries that facilitate interaction between PHP and the chosen DBMS can greatly enhance productivity.

Lastly, consider the long-term implications of your DBMS choice, such as licensing costs, compatibility with future technologies, and the potential need for migration. Some systems are open-source and free to use, while others may require licensing fees as your application grows. Furthermore, ensuring that the DBMS can accommodate future growth in data volume and user traffic is crucial. By carefully evaluating these considerations, career-changed professionals and students can make informed decisions that align with their goals and set a solid foundation for their PHP database endeavors.

Configuring Your Development Environment

When starting with PHP databases, configuring your development environment is a crucial first step. A well-set environment not only enhances productivity but also minimizes potential issues during development. The primary components of a PHP development environment typically include a web server, PHP itself, a database server, and a suitable code editor. This combination allows you to write, test, and debug PHP scripts that interact with databases efficiently.

To begin, you will need to choose a web server. Popular options include Apache and Nginx, which are widely used in the industry. Apache is particularly beginner-friendly due to its extensive documentation and large community support. Installing a package like XAMPP or MAMP can simplify this process, as these packages bundle Apache, PHP, and MySQL into a single installation. Once installed, you can easily configure these components to suit your development needs.

Next, ensuring that PHP is correctly installed is essential. PHP is a server-side scripting language that enables you to interact with databases. After installing your web server, verify that PHP is running by creating a simple PHP file with the command phpinfo(). This script will display your PHP configuration, including the version and enabled extensions. Familiarizing yourself with the PHP environment settings will help you troubleshoot issues and optimize performance later on.

Database configuration is the next critical step. MySQL is a common choice for beginners due to its ease of use and compatibility with PHP. After installing your web server and PHP, you can set up MySQL through the same package that installed Apache and PHP. Use tools like phpMyAdmin for a user-friendly interface to manage your databases. Creating a test database and practicing basic SQL commands can help you understand how PHP interacts with databases.

Finally, selecting a code editor that suits your workflow can significantly impact your development experience. Editors like Visual Studio Code, Sublime Text, or PHPStorm offer features such as syntax highlighting, debugging tools, and integration with version control systems. Experiment with different editors to find one that fits your needs best. Configuring your development environment effectively will provide you with a solid foundation as you delve into PHP and database management, paving the way for your learning and career growth.

Chapter 3: Basics of SQL

Introduction to SQL

Structured Query Language, commonly known as SQL, is a powerful tool for managing and manipulating relational databases. It serves as the standard language for database interaction, allowing users to create, modify, and query data stored in various database management systems. For those embarking on a journey in PHP and database development, understanding SQL is essential, as it forms the backbone of data handling in web applications. Whether you are a career changer or a student eager to learn, grasping the fundamentals of SQL provides a solid foundation for your database-related endeavors.

At its core, SQL enables users to perform a variety of operations on databases. These operations include creating new databases and tables, inserting data, updating existing records, and deleting data that is no longer needed. Additionally, SQL allows for data retrieval through complex queries that can filter, sort, and aggregate information based on specific criteria. This flexibility and power make SQL an indispensable skill for anyone looking to work with databases in conjunction with PHP, as it directly influences how data is accessed and manipulated within applications.

One of the reasons SQL remains prevalent in the tech industry is its ability to interact with various database management systems like MySQL, PostgreSQL, and

Microsoft SQL Server. Each of these systems may have unique features and optimizations, but they all adhere to the SQL standard, ensuring that the foundational commands and structure remain consistent. This consistency allows learners to transfer their knowledge across different platforms with relative ease, making SQL a versatile tool in a developer's toolkit.

As you embark on learning SQL, it is important to understand the basic syntax and commands that form the language's foundation. Key commands such as SELECT, INSERT, UPDATE, and DELETE will become familiar as you practice writing queries to interact with your database. Additionally, concepts such as database normalization, primary keys, and foreign keys will be introduced, providing a deeper understanding of how data is structured and related within a relational database. This foundational knowledge is crucial for building more complex applications and ensuring data integrity.

Finally, the practical application of SQL in conjunction with PHP cannot be overstated. As a server-side scripting language, PHP often works hand-in-hand with SQL to create dynamic web applications that respond to user input and display relevant data. By mastering SQL, you will unlock the potential to build robust, data-driven applications that meet real-world needs. This synergy between PHP and SQL not only enhances your programming skills but also prepares you for a rewarding career in web development and database management.

Common SQL Commands

SQL, or Structured Query Language, is the standard language used to communicate with relational database management systems. Understanding common SQL commands is essential for anyone looking to work with databases in PHP. These commands allow users to perform various operations, including retrieving, inserting, updating, and deleting data. The fundamental SQL commands include SELECT, INSERT, UPDATE, and DELETE, each serving a unique purpose in database management.

The SELECT command is one of the most widely used SQL commands, allowing users to query the database and retrieve specific data. By using SELECT, you can specify the columns you want to view, the table from which to pull the data, and any conditions that need to be met. For example, a simple query like SELECT * FROM users retrieves all data from the users table. This command can be tailored with WHERE clauses to filter results based on certain criteria, making it an invaluable tool for data analysis.

INSERT commands are used to add new records to a database table. When using INSERT, you specify the table and the values that correspond to each column. For example, INSERT INTO users (name, email) VALUES ('John Doe', 'john@example.com') adds a new user to the users table. This command is crucial for storing new information, whether it's user registrations or transaction records. Understanding how to properly format and execute INSERT statements is vital for maintaining an up-to-date database.

To modify existing records, the UPDATE command is employed. This command allows users to change data within a specified table. By using the UPDATE command along with the SET clause, you can specify which columns to change and their new values. For instance, the command UPDATE users SET email = 'john.doe@example.com' WHERE name = 'John Doe' updates the email address for a specific user. Mastering the UPDATE command is key to keeping your database accurate and reflective of any changes in user data or system requirements.

Finally, the DELETE command is utilized to remove records from a database. This command must be used with caution, as it permanently deletes data. A typical DELETE command would look like DELETE FROM users WHERE name = 'John Doe', which removes the user named John Doe from the users table. Understanding how to safely execute DELETE commands is essential for maintaining data integrity and ensuring that only the desired records are removed. Together, these common SQL commands form the foundation for interacting with databases in PHP, providing the tools necessary for effective data management.

Understanding Data Types

Data types are fundamental concepts that underpin all programming languages, including PHP. Understanding data types is essential for handling and manipulating data effectively within a database. In PHP, data types can be broadly categorized into scalar types, composite types, and special types. Scalar types include integers, floats, strings, and booleans, which represent single values. Composite types, such as arrays and objects, can store multiple values. Special types include resources and null, which have unique characteristics in programming. Recognizing these distinctions allows developers to choose the right data type for their specific needs, ultimately enhancing performance and efficiency.

In PHP, integers are whole numbers without decimal points, ranging from negative to positive values. They are often used for counting and indexing, making them a popular choice when working with loops or array positions. Floats, on the other hand, represent numbers with decimal points. This data type is essential when precision is necessary, such as in financial calculations. Strings are sequences of characters enclosed in quotes, used to represent text data. Booleans are particularly useful for making decisions in code, as they can only hold two values: true or false. Understanding these scalar types allows new learners to manipulate data effectively when interacting with a database.

Composite types, namely arrays and objects, offer more complex data structures that can hold multiple values or properties. Arrays can be indexed or associative, enabling users to store collections of data that can be accessed using keys or indices. For instance, an array might hold a list of user names or product prices. Objects represent instances of classes and encapsulate both data and behavior. They are especially useful in object-oriented programming, allowing for more organized and modular code. By mastering composite types, learners can create sophisticated data models that reflect real-world scenarios in their applications.

PHP also includes special data types that serve unique purposes. The resource type is used to reference external resources, such as database connections or file handles. This type is crucial for managing operations that require external data sources. The null type represents a variable with no value assigned, which can be useful for checking whether a variable has been initialized. Understanding these special types helps new learners identify when to use specific constructs, leading to clearer and more efficient code.

In conclusion, grasping the various data types in PHP is a vital step for anyone looking to work with databases. A solid foundation in scalar, composite, and special data types enables beginners to write effective code, optimize database interactions, and implement more complex logic within their applications. As career-changed professionals and students embark on their journey in PHP and database management, a thorough understanding of data types will empower them to tackle various challenges and enhance their programming skills.

Chapter 4: Connecting PHP to a Database

Using MySQLi

MySQLi, which stands for MySQL Improved, is a powerful extension of PHP that offers an enhanced way to interact with MySQL databases. It provides both procedural and object-oriented interfaces, allowing developers to choose the style that best suits their coding preferences. MySQLi is specifically designed to take advantage of the features of MySQL 4.1.3 and later, making it an ideal choice for modern web applications. For beginners, understanding how to use MySQLi effectively is crucial, as it lays the foundation for building dynamic, database-driven websites.

To get started with MySQLi, the first step is establishing a connection to the database. This can be done using the mysqli_connect() function in procedural style or by creating a new instance of the mysqli class in object-oriented style. Both approaches require parameters such as the server name, username, password, and database name. Once the connection is successfully established, it is essential to check for any errors that may have occurred during the process. This ensures that the application can handle issues gracefully, providing a better user experience.

Once connected, executing queries is the next step. MySQLi allows you to run various types of SQL statements, including SELECT, INSERT, UPDATE, and DELETE. For beginners, the mysqli_query() function is often the easiest way to execute a query in procedural style. In object-oriented style, you can use the query() method of the mysqli object. It is important to understand the difference between executing queries that return results, such as SELECT statements, and those that do not, like INSERT or DELETE statements. This distinction is crucial for handling returned data appropriately.

Retrieving data from the database is a critical aspect of using MySQLi. For SELECT queries, the mysqli_fetch_assoc() function allows you to fetch results as an associative array, making it easy to access column values by their names. Alternatively, mysqli_fetch_array() can be used to fetch results as both an associative and a numeric array. Understanding these methods enables beginners to manipulate and display data effectively. Additionally, it is important to properly free up resources using mysqli_free_result() after data retrieval to maintain optimal performance.

Finally, security is an essential consideration when using MySQLi. Beginners should be aware of the risks associated with SQL injection, a common attack vector where malicious input is used to manipulate SQL queries. To mitigate this risk, it is crucial to use prepared statements, which separate SQL logic from data inputs. MySQLi supports prepared statements, allowing developers to bind parameters securely, thus preventing unauthorized access to the database. Mastering MySQLi not only helps in building robust applications but also instills best practices in database management and security for new learners in the field.

Using PDO

Using PHP Data Objects (PDO) is essential for anyone looking to interact with databases in a secure and efficient manner. PDO is a database access layer that provides a uniform method of access to multiple databases. This abstraction allows developers to switch database systems with minimal changes to their code. For beginners, understanding how to use PDO is crucial as it forms the backbone of many PHP applications that require database interactions.

One of the primary advantages of PDO is its support for prepared statements. Prepared statements help prevent SQL injection attacks, which are a common security vulnerability in web applications. By using placeholders in SQL queries, developers can effectively separate the SQL logic from the data being processed. This not only enhances security but also improves performance, as the SQL statements are compiled only once and can be executed multiple times with different parameters.

To get started with PDO, the first step is to create a new PDO instance. This involves providing the Data Source Name (DSN), which specifies the database type and location, along with the username and password for authentication. Once the connection is established, developers can begin executing queries. Using the PDO methods, such as query(), prepare(), and execute(), allows for a streamlined approach to managing database operations. Understanding these methods is vital for beginners, as they form the core of interacting with databases through PDO.

Error handling in PDO is another important aspect that new learners should grasp. PDO offers multiple ways to handle errors, including exceptions. By setting the error mode attribute, developers can catch exceptions that occur during database operations, allowing for graceful handling of errors and improving the overall robustness of the application. This feature is particularly beneficial for beginners, as it encourages best practices in error management and debugging.

Finally, mastering PDO opens up opportunities for working with different database systems. Whether you are using MySQL, PostgreSQL, or SQLite, PDO provides a consistent interface that minimizes the need to learn different database APIs. This flexibility is especially valuable for career changers and students, as it allows them to focus on building applications rather than getting bogged down by database-specific syntax. By leveraging PDO, learners can build secure, efficient, and portable applications that can adapt to various database environments.

Error Handling in Database Connections

Error handling in database connections is a crucial aspect of developing robust PHP applications. When working with databases, various issues can arise, such as connection failures, authentication problems, or unexpected server responses. Understanding how to manage these errors effectively can prevent your application from crashing and provide a better user experience. Proper error handling allows developers to identify issues quickly and respond appropriately, ensuring that the application continues to function smoothly.

One of the foundational steps in error handling is to establish a clear strategy for how to manage errors during database connections. PHP offers several methods for handling errors, including using traditional error handling functions or implementing exception handling through try-catch blocks. By utilizing these techniques, developers can catch errors at the moment they occur and respond without disrupting the user experience. This is particularly important in production environments where users may be interacting with the application in real-time.

When using PDO (PHP Data Objects) for database connections, it is advisable to set the error mode to exception. This way, any database errors will be thrown as exceptions that can be caught and handled gracefully. For instance, if a connection to the database fails, instead of allowing the script to terminate abruptly, the developer can catch the exception and display a user-friendly error message or redirect the user to a troubleshooting page. This practice not only improves the user experience but also aids developers in diagnosing issues during the development phase.

Additionally, logging errors is an essential component of effective error handling. By logging errors to a file or a monitoring system, developers can maintain a record of what went wrong and when. This information is invaluable for troubleshooting and can help identify recurring issues that may need to be addressed. PHP provides various logging libraries and functions that can be integrated into applications to facilitate this process. Consistent logging practices empower developers to enhance the stability and reliability of their applications over time.

Finally, it is important to test error handling thoroughly in different scenarios. Developers should simulate various failure conditions, such as incorrect credentials or database server downtime, to ensure that their error handling logic is robust. By testing these scenarios, developers can verify that their applications respond appropriately and that users receive helpful feedback when issues arise. This proactive approach to error handling not only strengthens applications but also builds confidence for developers who are transitioning into PHP database management.

Chapter 5: Performing CRUD Operations

Creating Data

Creating data in a database is a fundamental operation that every beginner in PHP and database management must master. This process involves inserting new records into a database table, which can be accomplished using SQL commands and PHP scripts. The most common command for this operation is the INSERT statement, which allows users to specify the table where they want to add data and the values that correspond to each column. Understanding how to structure this command correctly is essential for ensuring data integrity and preventing errors during data entry.

When working with PHP, the integration with a database is typically achieved through the use of the PDO (PHP Data Objects) extension or MySQLi (MySQL Improved). Both of these methods provide secure ways to connect to a database and execute SQL queries. For beginners, PDO is often recommended due to its flexibility and support for multiple database systems. Establishing a connection involves creating a new PDO instance, passing in the database connection parameters, and handling any exceptions that may arise. Proper error handling is crucial to provide feedback and maintain the robustness of the application.

Once a connection is established, inserting data can be accomplished using prepared statements. Prepared statements are a powerful feature that helps prevent SQL injection attacks, a common security vulnerability in web applications. By using placeholders in SQL queries, developers can ensure that user input is safely passed to the database. This approach not only enhances security but also improves performance, especially when executing similar queries multiple times. Beginners should focus on understanding how to prepare statements and bind parameters effectively to create secure and efficient data insertion processes.

In addition to inserting single records, it is also possible to insert multiple records at once using a single SQL statement. This can be done by specifying multiple sets of values in the INSERT statement, which reduces the number of database calls and improves performance. Learning how to batch insert data is particularly useful when dealing with large datasets or when migrating data from one system to another. Beginners should practice forming these queries and consider the implications of transaction management, ensuring that all data is inserted correctly or rolled back in case of an error.

Lastly, after successfully inserting data, it is essential to verify that the operation was completed successfully. This can be done by checking the number of affected rows or querying the database to confirm the new records exist. Incorporating this validation step into your workflow not only reinforces good programming practices but also helps in debugging and maintaining the integrity of your application. As you continue to create and manipulate data within your PHP applications, remember that mastering these foundational skills will pave the way for more complex database interactions and ultimately lead to greater proficiency in PHP and database management.

Reading Data

Reading data from a database is a fundamental skill in PHP that allows developers to retrieve and manipulate information effectively. This process typically involves establishing a connection to the database, executing a query, and then processing the results. For beginners, understanding these steps is crucial as they form the backbone of data-driven applications. PHP provides various methods for interacting with databases, but using the MySQLi or PDO extensions is highly recommended for their flexibility and security features.

To start reading data, you first need to establish a connection to your database. This is done using either the MySQLi extension or the PDO extension. With MySQLi, you can connect using procedural or object-oriented styles. For instance, you might use the mysqli_connect function, providing it with your database host, username, password, and database name. Similarly, with PDO, you create a new PDO object and pass in the Data Source Name (DSN), username, and password. A successful connection will allow you to perform database operations, including reading data.

Once the connection is established, the next step is to construct a SQL query. SQL, or Structured Query Language, is the language used to interact with databases. A simple SELECT statement can be used to retrieve specific columns from a table. For example, a query like "SELECT * FROM users" retrieves all records from the users table. It is essential to formulate your queries carefully to avoid common pitfalls, such as SQL injection, which can compromise your database security. Utilizing prepared statements, especially when using PDO, is a best practice that helps mitigate these risks.

After executing the query, the results need to be processed. Depending on the method used, the way results are fetched will vary. MySQLi provides functions like mysqli_fetch_assoc and mysqli_fetch_array, while PDO offers methods such as fetch and fetchAll. These functions allow you to retrieve data in various formats, such as associative arrays or objects, making it easier to work with the data in your application. Understanding how to navigate and manipulate these results is vital for effective data handling in PHP.

Finally, don't forget to close the database connection after your operations are complete. This is an important step to free up resources and maintain performance. In MySQLi, you can simply call the mysqli_close function, whereas in PDO, the connection is automatically closed when the object is destroyed. Additionally, implementing error handling throughout your data reading process ensures that your application can gracefully manage issues such as connection failures or SQL errors, providing a smoother user experience. By mastering these techniques, beginners can confidently handle data reading in PHP, setting a strong foundation for their database-driven applications.

Updating Data

Updating data in a database is a fundamental operation that allows users to modify existing records. In PHP, this process typically involves the use of SQL commands, specifically the UPDATE statement. Understanding how to properly execute an update is crucial, as it directly impacts the integrity of your data. The update operation is commonly utilized when there is a need to correct information or when changes to data are necessary due to external factors.

To begin updating data, it is essential to establish a connection to the database using PHP. This is achieved through the use of the PDO (PHP Data Objects) extension or the MySQLi (MySQL Improved) extension. Both methods offer a secure way to interact with the database. Once a connection is established, the next step is to write an effective SQL UPDATE statement. This statement typically includes the name of the table you wish to update, the columns to be modified, and the condition indicating which records should be affected. Utilizing conditions, or WHERE clauses, is critical to ensure that only the intended records are modified.

When constructing an UPDATE statement, it's important to be mindful of SQL injection vulnerabilities. To safeguard your application, you should use prepared statements, which separate SQL logic from data inputs. This practice not only enhances security but also improves performance by allowing the database to optimize repeated queries. For instance, using placeholders in your SQL statements ensures that user inputs are treated as data rather than executable code, thus mitigating the risks associated with malicious inputs.

After crafting the SQL statement, executing it with PHP is straightforward. The execution can be done using the execute() method for prepared statements. It is also advisable to check for successful execution by evaluating the return value of the execution method. If the update operation fails, handling errors gracefully is essential to maintain a good user experience. Providing feedback or logging errors can help identify issues during development and debugging phases.

Finally, once the data has been successfully updated, it is a good practice to confirm the changes by querying the database to retrieve the updated records. This check ensures that the operation performed as expected and that the data integrity is maintained. Regularly reviewing and testing your database interactions will solidify your understanding and competence in handling data updates, making you a more proficient PHP developer. As you progress in your learning journey, mastering data manipulation operations like updating will be invaluable in building dynamic web applications.

Deleting Data

Deleting data is a fundamental operation in database management that every developer must understand, especially those working with PHP and relational databases like MySQL. This operation allows users to remove unwanted or outdated records from a database, ensuring that the data remains relevant and manageable. The DELETE statement is the primary means of accomplishing this task, and it can be executed through various methods in PHP to maintain the integrity of the database while effectively managing data.

To delete data from a database using PHP, you must first establish a connection to the database using the mysqli or PDO extensions. After successfully connecting, you can formulate a DELETE query. A typical DELETE statement follows the structure: DELETE FROM table_name WHERE condition. The condition is crucial as it specifies which record(s) to remove; omitting it can result in unintended data loss. For instance, if you were to delete all records from a "users" table without a WHERE clause, it would remove every entry, potentially leading to significant data loss.

Error handling is an essential aspect of deleting data. It is vital to check for the success of the deletion operation to ensure that the intended records were removed and to handle any potential issues gracefully. Using the mysqli or PDO methods, you can check the result of the execution to see how many rows were affected. This feedback allows developers to confirm that the operation was performed correctly and provides an opportunity to implement rollback mechanisms if necessary.

In addition to the basic DELETE operation, it is often prudent to implement additional safeguards when deleting data. For example, soft deletes can be used instead of hard deletes, where a record is marked as deleted without actually removing it from the database. This approach can be particularly useful for maintaining historical data or allowing for easy recovery of mistakenly deleted entries. Implementing a "deleted" status column can help manage this process, where the application logic is adjusted to ignore records marked as deleted during standard queries.

Understanding the implications of deleting data is crucial for maintaining data integrity and application functionality. It is essential to consider the relationships between tables in a relational database, as deleting records in one table may affect related records in another. For example, if a user is deleted from a "users" table, their associated orders in an "orders" table may also need to be addressed. Employing foreign key constraints with cascading deletes or updating related records accordingly can help maintain referential integrity in the database. By mastering these concepts, beginners can confidently navigate the complexities of data deletion within their PHP applications.

Chapter 6: Advanced SQL Queries

Joining Tables

Joining tables is a fundamental concept in relational databases that allows you to combine rows from two or more tables based on a related column. This operation is crucial for retrieving meaningful data that is spread across different tables. In PHP, you can perform joins using SQL queries, which enable you to write code that fetches data efficiently. Understanding how to join tables will empower you to create more complex and functional applications, as it allows for a more organized approach to data management.

There are several types of joins in SQL, each serving different purposes. The most common types are INNER JOIN, LEFT JOIN, RIGHT JOIN, and FULL OUTER JOIN. An INNER JOIN returns only the rows that have matching values in both tables, making it useful when you need data that exists in both sources. A LEFT JOIN, on the other hand, returns all records from the left table and the matched records from the right table, with NULLs for unmatched rows. This approach is particularly helpful when you want to include all entries from one table, regardless of whether they have related entries in another.

To illustrate how joins work, consider a database with two tables: one for customers and another for orders. If you want to retrieve a list of customers along with their orders, you would use an INNER JOIN to connect the two tables through a common column, such as customer_id. This unified dataset would allow you to see which customers have placed orders and to what extent. Conversely, using a LEFT JOIN would allow you to display all customers, even those who have not placed any orders, along with their corresponding order details where available.

Implementing joins in PHP is straightforward using the PDO (PHP Data Objects) extension, which provides a consistent method for accessing databases. After establishing a connection to your database, you can write your SQL query with the appropriate join type. For example, using a prepared statement helps prevent SQL injection, ensuring your application remains secure. Once the query is executed, you can fetch the results and display them in your application, enabling users to interact with the combined data seamlessly.

Mastering the art of joining tables is essential for any developer working with PHP and databases. By learning to effectively combine data from multiple sources, you enhance the functionality of your applications and provide richer user experiences. As you continue your journey in PHP and database management, practicing various join types will build your confidence and deepen your understanding, equipping you with the skills necessary for real-world scenarios.

Using Subqueries

Using subqueries is a powerful technique in SQL that allows you to perform more complex queries by nesting one query within another. This can be particularly useful when you need to retrieve data based on the results of another query. For beginners learning PHP databases, understanding subqueries can enhance your ability to manipulate and extract information from your data effectively. A subquery is enclosed in parentheses and can be used in various clauses of a SQL statement, such as SELECT, INSERT, UPDATE, and DELETE.

There are two main types of subqueries: single-row and multiple-row subqueries. A single-row subquery returns only one row of data, while a multiple-row subquery can return multiple rows. When using a single-row subquery, you can utilize operators like '=', '<', or '>' to compare values. For instance, if you want to find employees who earn more than the average salary, you could write a subquery that first calculates the average salary and then use that result in the main query to filter employees accordingly. This makes your SQL statements more dynamic and adaptable.

Subqueries can also be used in the WHERE clause to filter results based on related data. For example, if you want to find all customers who have placed orders, you can use a subquery to select customer IDs from the orders table and then filter the customers based on those IDs. This allows you to efficiently join data from multiple tables without needing to perform explicit JOIN operations. Such flexibility is beneficial for beginners as it simplifies the SQL syntax while still allowing for complex data retrieval tasks.

Another important aspect of subqueries is their use in the FROM clause. This enables you to treat the results of a subquery as if it were a table, allowing for more intricate data manipulation. For example, you might create a subquery that aggregates sales data by product, and then use that aggregated result to further analyze trends or generate reports. This can be particularly useful in scenarios where you need to summarize or transform data before conducting additional queries.

When using subqueries, it is essential to keep performance in mind. While subqueries can make your SQL statements more readable and manageable, they can also lead to slower execution times if not used judiciously. Beginners should practice writing both subqueries and equivalent JOIN statements to understand the trade-offs in performance and readability. As you gain experience, you will become adept at choosing the right approach for your specific data retrieval needs.

Aggregate Functions

Aggregate functions are essential tools in SQL that allow users to perform calculations on multiple rows of data and return a single value. These functions are particularly useful when working with large datasets, enabling users to summarize information efficiently. Common aggregate functions include COUNT, SUM, AVG, MIN, and MAX. Each of these functions serves a unique purpose, facilitating different types of data analysis and reporting, which is crucial for decision-making in various applications.

The COUNT function is one of the most straightforward aggregate functions. It returns the number of rows that match a specified criterion. For instance, if a developer wants to know how many users registered on a website in a given week, they can use the COUNT function in their SQL query. This function can also count distinct values, which is useful when needing to identify unique entries, such as the number of unique products sold in a specific timeframe.

SUM, another widely used aggregate function, adds together the values of a specified column. This function is particularly advantageous in financial applications where totals need to be calculated, such as total sales or total expenses. By using the SUM function, developers can quickly generate reports that provide insights into financial performance over different periods, helping businesses make informed decisions based on their data.

The AVG function calculates the average value of a specified column, providing insight into overall trends and performance. For example, a company might use AVG to determine the average sales per transaction over a month, helping them assess the effectiveness of marketing strategies. Understanding average values is critical for evaluating performance metrics and making adjustments where necessary, allowing businesses to enhance their operational efficiency.

In addition to these functions, MIN and MAX can be utilized to find the smallest and largest values in a dataset, respectively. These functions are beneficial in scenarios where understanding extremes is necessary, such as identifying the highest sale in a quarter or the lowest temperature recorded in a dataset. By leveraging these aggregate functions, PHP developers can enhance their applications, ensuring they provide meaningful insights from the data stored within databases, ultimately leading to better strategic decisions and outcomes.

Chapter 7: Securing Your Database

Understanding SQL Injection

SQL injection is a type of security vulnerability that allows an attacker to interfere with the queries that an application makes to its database. This occurs when user input is improperly filtered for string literal escape characters embedded in SQL statements. As a result, an attacker can manipulate the SQL query by injecting malicious code, which may lead to unauthorized access to sensitive data, data corruption, or even complete system compromise. Understanding SQL injection is crucial for anyone working with databases, especially those using PHP, as it is one of the most common security threats faced by web applications.

The mechanics of SQL injection are relatively straightforward. When a web application incorporates user input directly into SQL queries without proper validation or escaping, it becomes vulnerable. For example, consider a typical login form where a user enters their username and password. If the application constructs a query like "SELECT * FROM users WHERE username = '$username' AND password = '$password'", an attacker could input a specially crafted string that alters the intended logic of the query. This could allow the attacker to bypass authentication or extract sensitive information from the database.

To illustrate, suppose an attacker enters "admin' OR '1'='1" as the username and any password. The resulting SQL query would become "SELECT * FROM users WHERE username = 'admin' OR '1'='1' AND password = 'any_password'". Since '1'='1' is always true, this query would return a valid user record, potentially granting the attacker access to the application as an administrator. Such examples highlight the critical need for developers to understand how SQL injection works and the potential consequences of neglecting input validation.

Preventing SQL injection requires a proactive approach to coding practices. One of the most effective methods is using prepared statements with parameterized queries. This technique separates SQL code from user input, ensuring that any data provided by users cannot alter the structure of the SQL command. In PHP, using PDO (PHP Data Objects) or MySQLi (MySQL Improved) allows developers to implement prepared statements easily, thereby significantly reducing the risk of SQL injection. Additionally, employing proper input validation and sanitization measures can further enhance the security of an application.

In conclusion, understanding SQL injection is essential for anyone involved in PHP database development. By recognizing how SQL injection works and implementing preventative measures such as prepared statements, developers can protect their applications from this widespread vulnerability. As the threat landscape continues to evolve, staying informed about security best practices is vital for safeguarding sensitive data and maintaining the integrity of web applications. By prioritizing security from the outset, new learners in PHP databases can build robust applications that stand up against potential attacks.

Best Practices for Data Security

In today's digital landscape, data security is paramount, especially for those venturing into PHP databases. As career-changed professionals and students of all ages begin their journey in this field, understanding best practices for data security is essential. Establishing a solid foundation in data security not only protects sensitive information but also fosters trust with users and clients.

One of the foremost best practices in securing PHP databases is to implement robust authentication mechanisms. This includes using strong passwords and multi-factor authentication to prevent unauthorized access. Encouraging users to create complex passwords and regularly update them can significantly reduce the risk of breaches. Additionally, limiting login attempts and locking out users after a set number of failed attempts can help thwart brute force attacks. By incorporating these strategies, developers can create a more secure environment for their applications.

Data validation and sanitization are critical steps in maintaining the integrity of information within PHP databases. Input validation ensures that only properly formatted data is accepted, while sanitization involves cleaning data to remove any harmful elements. This practice is particularly important to prevent SQL injection attacks, where malicious users attempt to manipulate database queries. Employing prepared statements and parameterized queries in PHP can effectively mitigate these risks. By prioritizing data validation and sanitization, developers can safeguard their applications against common vulnerabilities.

Regularly updating software and dependencies is another vital aspect of data security. Outdated software can harbor known vulnerabilities that cybercriminals exploit. It is crucial to stay informed about the latest security patches and updates for PHP, as well as any libraries and frameworks in use. Implementing a schedule for routine updates and monitoring security advisories can help maintain a secure environment. This proactive approach not only protects the database but also ensures compliance with industry standards and regulations.

Lastly, implementing proper access control measures is essential for limiting exposure to sensitive data. This includes assigning user roles and permissions based on the principle of least privilege, where users only have access to the data necessary for their tasks. Additionally, regularly reviewing and auditing access logs can help identify any unauthorized access attempts. By maintaining strict access controls, developers can minimize the risk of data breaches and ensure that sensitive information remains protected.

In conclusion, understanding and implementing best practices for data security in PHP databases is crucial for beginners. By focusing on authentication, data validation, software updates, and access control, new learners can build secure applications that protect sensitive information. Establishing these practices early in their careers will not only enhance their skills but also prepare them for the challenges of the evolving digital landscape.

User Authentication and Authorization

User authentication and authorization are critical components in web development, ensuring that only legitimate users gain access to specific resources and functionalities within an application. Authentication is the process of verifying a user's identity, usually through a username and password. In PHP, this can be achieved by creating a login system that interacts with a database to check user credentials against stored data. Upon successful authentication, the user can be granted access to various functionalities based on their identity.

Once a user is authenticated, the next step is authorization, which determines what an authenticated user is allowed to do. This involves defining user roles and permissions within the application. For instance, in a content management system, an administrator might have permission to create, edit, and delete posts, while regular users may only have the ability to comment on existing posts. Implementing a robust authorization mechanism helps prevent unauthorized access and ensures that users can only perform actions that align with their roles.

To implement user authentication in PHP, developers typically use sessions to maintain user state after they log in. When a user logs in, their information is usually stored in a session variable, which can then be accessed throughout the application. This allows the application to remember that the user is logged in as they navigate between different pages. It is essential to secure session management, employing techniques such as regenerating session IDs upon login and setting appropriate session timeouts to reduce the risk of session hijacking.

For authorization, developers can use role-based access control (RBAC) models, where each user is assigned a role that corresponds to a set of permissions. This can be implemented in PHP by creating a database table that defines roles and their associated permissions. When a user attempts to perform an action, the application checks their role against the required permissions. This approach not only simplifies the management of user rights but also enhances security by clearly delineating what each user can access within the application.

In conclusion, user authentication and authorization are foundational elements in securing PHP applications. By implementing these processes thoughtfully, developers can ensure that their applications are not only user-friendly but also secure against unauthorized access. As career-changed professionals and students begin their journey into PHP databases, understanding and applying these concepts is essential for creating robust and secure web applications. Mastering user authentication and authorization will ultimately empower developers to build applications that protect user data and maintain integrity in their operations.

Chapter 8: Working with PHP Frameworks

Overview of PHP Frameworks

PHP frameworks serve as essential tools for developers, streamlining the process of building robust web applications. By providing a structured foundation, these frameworks enable developers to write cleaner, more maintainable code while adhering to best practices. The adoption of a framework typically results in increased productivity, as many of the repetitive tasks associated with web development are automated. This is particularly beneficial for career-changed professionals and students who may be new to programming, as it allows them to focus on learning the core concepts of web development without getting overwhelmed by the complexities of coding from scratch.

Among the various PHP frameworks available, Laravel has gained significant popularity due to its elegant syntax and extensive features. It offers a powerful ORM (Object-Relational Mapping) called Eloquent, which simplifies database interactions, making it easier for beginners to manage data without requiring in-depth knowledge of SQL. Laravel also includes built-in functionalities for routing, authentication, and caching, enabling new developers to create fully functional applications more rapidly. Additionally, the vast Laravel community provides ample resources, tutorials, and support, which further aids learners in overcoming challenges they may encounter during their development journey.

Another notable framework is Symfony, which is renowned for its flexibility and scalability. It is designed for larger applications, making it a great choice for developers who anticipate growth in their projects. Symfony's modular structure allows developers to use only the components they need, which can lead to more efficient applications. For those new to PHP development, Symfony may present a steeper learning curve compared to Laravel, but its comprehensive documentation and active community can help bridge that gap. Understanding Symfony can provide learners with valuable insights into enterprise-level application development.

CodeIgniter is another popular PHP framework favored for its simplicity and speed. It is lightweight and easy to install, making it an attractive option for beginners. CodeIgniter does not impose strict coding rules, allowing developers the freedom to write code in a way that feels comfortable to them. This flexibility makes it an ideal starting point for those who are just beginning to explore web development with PHP. Its straightforward approach ensures that new learners can quickly grasp the essentials of framework-based development without the distractions of complex configurations.

Finally, there is Yii, a high-performance framework that excels in building large-scale applications. Yii is known for its powerful caching capabilities, which can significantly enhance performance, making it suitable for applications with heavy traffic. It also comes with a robust set of tools for database management, which is particularly relevant for the target audience of this book. For those transitioning into web development, understanding Yii can provide a solid foundation in building efficient and scalable applications while also reinforcing key database concepts. By exploring these frameworks, learners can choose the one that best fits their project needs and personal learning style.

Using Laravel for Database Interaction

Laravel is a powerful PHP framework that simplifies the process of database interaction through its elegant syntax and robust features. For those new to PHP and databases, Laravel provides an accessible way to manage database operations without the complexity often associated with traditional SQL queries. Its built-in Eloquent ORM (Object-Relational Mapping) allows developers to interact with the database using object-oriented syntax, making code easier to read and maintain. This abstraction layer helps beginners focus on building applications without getting bogged down in intricate SQL details.

One of the standout features of Laravel is its migration system, which allows developers to define and share database schemas in a version-controlled manner. Migrations are essentially version control for databases, enabling teams to manage changes collaboratively. New learners can create, modify, or rollback database structures effortlessly. This is particularly beneficial for career changers who may not be familiar with database management best practices, as it provides a structured way to handle schema changes and ensures consistency across different development environments.

Laravel also simplifies data retrieval with its fluent query builder. Beginners can execute complex queries without needing extensive knowledge of SQL syntax. The query builder allows for chaining methods, which leads to clearer and more intuitive code. For example, fetching records from a database can be done in a few simple lines, making it accessible for those who may feel overwhelmed by more verbose SQL commands. This ease of use helps students and professionals quickly grasp the fundamentals of database interaction, enabling them to focus on application logic instead.

Error handling and database transactions are critical aspects of database interaction, and Laravel excels in these areas. The framework provides robust tools for managing exceptions and rolling back transactions when necessary. For new learners, understanding how to handle errors gracefully is vital for building reliable applications. Laravel's built-in support for transactions ensures that a series of database operations either complete successfully or revert to their previous state, preventing data corruption. This feature instills confidence in developers as they learn to build applications that are resilient and maintain data integrity.

Finally, Laravel's community and ecosystem offer an abundance of resources for beginners. With extensive documentation, tutorials, and forums, learners can easily find help and support as they navigate their database journey. Additionally, Laravel integrates seamlessly with various database systems, including MySQL, PostgreSQL, and SQLite, making it versatile for different project requirements. For career changers and students alike, leveraging Laravel for database interaction not only enhances their PHP skills but also prepares them for real-world development challenges, making it an invaluable tool in their learning arsenal.

Using CodeIgniter for Simplified Development

CodeIgniter is a powerful PHP framework that is designed to facilitate the development of web applications by providing a simplified coding experience. Its lightweight structure and straightforward setup make it an ideal choice for beginners who are transitioning into PHP development. With CodeIgniter, developers can focus more on building robust applications rather than getting bogged down by the complexities often associated with other frameworks. This simplicity is particularly beneficial for career changers and students who may not have an extensive background in programming but are eager to learn and develop practical skills quickly.

One of the key features of CodeIgniter is its Model-View-Controller (MVC) architecture, which separates application logic from the user interface. This separation allows developers to manage their code more efficiently and makes it easier to maintain and update applications over time. For new learners, understanding the MVC pattern is crucial, as it is a widely used design pattern in modern web development. By using CodeIgniter, beginners can grasp the principles of MVC while simultaneously working on real-world projects that require database interactions, making the learning process both engaging and practical.

CodeIgniter also provides a rich set of libraries and helpers that streamline common tasks, such as form validation, session management, and database interactions. These built-in functionalities significantly reduce the amount of code that developers need to write, allowing them to achieve more with less effort. For students and career changers, this means that they can create fully functional web applications without having to reinvent the wheel. Additionally, CodeIgniter's clear documentation and active community support make it easier for new developers to find solutions to common problems, fostering a more supportive learning environment.

Another advantage of using CodeIgniter is its compatibility with various database systems, including MySQL, PostgreSQL, and SQLite. This flexibility allows learners to experiment with different database technologies without being tied to a specific platform. Understanding how to interact with databases is a crucial skill for anyone venturing into PHP development, and CodeIgniter simplifies this process through its intuitive database abstraction layer. As learners build their skills in PHP and databases, they can confidently switch between different database systems, gaining a broader understanding of how web applications handle data.

In conclusion, CodeIgniter serves as an excellent starting point for those new to PHP and database development. Its lightweight framework, adherence to the MVC design pattern, extensive libraries, and database compatibility make it an ideal choice for students and professionals looking to enter the tech field. By utilizing CodeIgniter, learners can focus on acquiring essential programming skills while building practical applications that demonstrate their capabilities. This hands-on approach not only enhances their learning experience but also equips them with the tools they need to succeed in a competitive job market.

Chapter 9: Debugging and Testing

Common Database Errors

Common database errors can significantly impede development and learning for those new to PHP and database management. Understanding these errors is essential for effectively troubleshooting issues and ensuring smooth operations in projects. This subchapter will explore some of the most frequently encountered database errors, their causes, and how to address them, providing valuable insights for both career changers and students.

One of the most common errors is the "Connection Failed" error, which occurs when PHP is unable to establish a connection with the database server. This issue can arise due to incorrect database credentials, such as a wrong username or password, or an incorrect hostname or port number. It's important for beginners to double-check these details in their configuration files. Additionally, server issues, such as the database server being down or network connectivity problems, can also lead to this error. Ensuring that the database server is operational and accessible is crucial for successful connection.

Another frequent error is the "SQL Syntax Error," which typically arises from mistakes in the SQL statements being executed. This can occur due to typos, missing commas, or incorrect use of SQL keywords. For new learners, understanding the structure and syntax of SQL is vital. Debugging SQL queries can involve breaking them down into smaller parts and testing each component to isolate the issue. Utilizing tools like database management systems can also aid in identifying syntax errors as they often provide error messages indicating the problematic part of the query.

The "Data Type Mismatch" error is another common issue, especially when inserting or updating data in the database. This error occurs when the data being provided does not match the expected data type defined in the database schema. For instance, attempting to insert a string into an integer field will trigger this error. Beginners should familiarize themselves with the data types used in their databases and ensure that the data being processed matches these definitions. Proper validation of user inputs can also prevent such mismatches.

Additionally, "Permission Denied" errors can prevent users from executing certain database operations. This typically happens when the database user does not have the necessary privileges to perform specific actions, such as SELECT, INSERT, UPDATE, or DELETE. Understanding user roles and permissions is essential for both development and security. Beginners should learn how to configure user privileges appropriately within their database to avoid these errors. Regularly reviewing and managing database permissions is a best practice that can help maintain a secure and functional database environment.

In summary, recognizing and addressing common database errors is crucial for anyone starting with PHP and database management. By understanding connection issues, SQL syntax errors, data type mismatches, and permission problems, new learners can develop their troubleshooting skills and enhance their proficiency. This knowledge not only facilitates smoother development processes but also empowers individuals to tackle challenges confidently as they progress in their careers or studies.

Debugging Techniques in PHP

Debugging is an essential skill for anyone working with PHP, especially when dealing with databases. Effective debugging techniques help identify and resolve errors that can arise during development. One of the first steps in debugging PHP code is to enable error reporting. By setting the error reporting level in your PHP scripts, you can display warnings, notices, and fatal errors directly in the browser. This immediate feedback is invaluable for beginners as it highlights issues in real time, allowing for quicker resolution. Adjusting the error reporting level can be done with the function error_reporting(E_ALL); along with ini_set('display_errors', 1); to ensure that all errors are visible.

Another vital technique is the use of debugging tools and development environments. Tools such as Xdebug provide advanced debugging capabilities, including stack traces and breakpoint management. These features allow developers to inspect variables at different execution points and understand the flow of their code better. Integrated Development Environments (IDEs) like PhpStorm or Visual Studio Code also come equipped with debugging tools that streamline the debugging process. By utilizing these tools, developers can step through their code line by line, making it easier to identify where things are going wrong.

Logging is another effective debugging technique that can be particularly useful when working with databases. By implementing logging, you can track the execution of your scripts and record any errors that occur. This approach allows you to maintain a record of issues that may not be immediately visible during development. PHP provides built-in functions such as error_log() to write error messages to a specified log file. This method not only captures errors but can also help in monitoring database queries, making it easier to diagnose performance issues or unexpected behavior in your database interactions.

In addition to these techniques, effective debugging also involves writing clean and maintainable code. Adopting practices such as using meaningful variable names, breaking down complex functions into smaller, more manageable pieces, and commenting on your code can significantly ease the debugging process. When code is well-structured, it becomes easier to identify logical errors or incorrect assumptions. Additionally, using version control systems like Git can help track changes over time, making it possible to revert to earlier versions of your code if a new bug is introduced.

Finally, seeking help from online communities and resources can be a valuable part of the debugging process. Forums, discussion boards, and platforms like Stack Overflow are excellent places to ask questions and share experiences with fellow developers. Many common issues have already been encountered and resolved by others, so leveraging these resources can save you time and frustration. As you engage with these communities, remember that debugging is not just about fixing errors; it's also about developing a deeper understanding of PHP and database interactions, which will enhance your overall programming skills.

Writing Tests for Database Interactions

Writing tests for database interactions is a crucial step in ensuring the reliability and correctness of your PHP applications. When developing applications that rely on databases, the potential for errors increases significantly. Testing helps to identify issues before they make it into production, allowing developers to catch bugs early and ensure that their applications perform as expected. In this subchapter, we will explore the importance of testing, types of tests you can write, and best practices to follow when creating these tests.

One of the primary types of tests to consider is unit testing. Unit tests focus on individual components of your application, isolating each function or method to verify its behavior. When it comes to database interactions, unit tests can be designed to check whether your queries return the expected results. This can be achieved by mocking database connections and simulating the expected outcomes. By using tools such as PHPUnit, you can create a suite of unit tests that verify your database functions without needing to interact with the actual database. This makes your tests faster and more reliable, as they are not dependent on the database state.

Another important aspect of testing database interactions is integration testing. While unit tests focus on isolated components, integration tests examine how different parts of the application work together, particularly when it comes to database interactions. This type of testing is essential for identifying issues that may arise from the interaction between your PHP code and the database, such as incorrect data retrieval or failure to handle errors gracefully. Integration tests can be executed against a test database, allowing you to validate that your application behaves correctly in a realistic environment while safeguarding your production data.

When writing tests for database interactions, it is crucial to follow best practices to ensure that your tests are effective and maintainable. One key practice is to use a separate testing database, which prevents your tests from affecting the production data. You should also ensure that your tests are idempotent, meaning that they can be run multiple times without adverse effects. This is particularly important for database tests, as they may alter data. Additionally, consider using transactions to wrap your tests, allowing you to roll back changes after each test run. This approach guarantees a clean state for your database, making it easier to run tests consistently.

Lastly, documentation and continuous integration play a vital role in maintaining a robust testing strategy. As you write tests for your database interactions, document the purpose and functionality of each test case. This will help other developers understand the intent behind your tests and make it easier to expand the test suite in the future. Integrating your tests into a continuous integration pipeline allows you to automatically run your test suite whenever changes are made to the codebase, ensuring that any issues are caught promptly. By adopting these practices, you will enhance the quality of your PHP applications and ensure that your database interactions remain reliable.

Chapter 10: Real-World Applications

Building a Simple Web Application

Building a simple web application is a foundational step for anyone looking to dive into the world of PHP databases. A web application typically consists of a user interface, server-side logic, and a database to store and manage data. In this subchapter, we will walk through the essential components required to create a basic web application, focusing on the integration of PHP and a database system. This process will help you understand how data flows in a web environment and how PHP interacts with databases.

The first step in building a simple web application is setting up your development environment. This includes installing a local server environment like XAMPP or MAMP, which allows you to run PHP and manage MySQL databases locally. Once your environment is set up, you can create a directory for your project. This directory will house all your files, including HTML, CSS, JavaScript, and PHP files. Understanding how to organize these files is crucial as it will help you maintain and scale your application in the future.

Next, you'll want to create a basic user interface. This can be done using HTML and CSS to structure and style your web pages. Start by creating an index.php file, which will serve as the entry point for your application.

Inside this file, you can create a simple form that allows users to input data, such as their name and email address. This data will eventually be sent to the server for processing. Remember to utilize HTML form elements effectively and ensure that your layout is user-friendly and visually appealing.

Once your front-end is set up, it's time to dive into the back-end logic using PHP. You will write scripts that handle form submissions and interact with your database. This involves connecting to your MySQL database using PHP's PDO or MySQLi extensions. After establishing a connection, you can write SQL queries to insert, update, or retrieve data based on user input. It's essential to validate and sanitize any data before it is sent to the database to prevent SQL injection attacks and ensure data integrity.

Finally, testing and debugging are critical components of building any web application. After integrating the front-end and back-end, test your application thoroughly to ensure that all functionalities work as expected. Check for issues like form validation errors, database connection problems, and user experience flaws. Utilize browser developer tools and PHP error reporting to identify and fix any bugs. Once your application is functioning smoothly, you can consider deploying it to a live server, allowing users to access it from anywhere. Building a simple web application serves as a stepping stone into the more complex world of PHP and databases, equipping you with essential skills for further development.

Integrating Third-Party APIs

Integrating third-party APIs into your PHP applications can significantly enhance functionality and user experience. APIs, or Application Programming Interfaces, allow your application to communicate with external services, enabling you to leverage pre-built features such as payment processing, social media integration, or data retrieval from various sources. This subchapter will explore the process of integrating third-party APIs, focusing on the practical steps and considerations for beginners.

To start, it is essential to understand the basics of how APIs work. Most APIs utilize HTTP requests to send and receive data, typically formatted in JSON or XML. When integrating a third-party API, you will first need to register for an API key, which acts as a unique identifier for your application. This key is often required for authentication, ensuring that only authorized users can access the API's features. Familiarizing yourself with the API documentation is crucial, as it provides detailed information on available endpoints, request methods, and data formats.

Once you have your API key and have reviewed the documentation, the next step is to make a request to the API using PHP. This can be accomplished using various methods, including cURL or the built-in file_get_contents function. Using cURL is often preferred due to its flexibility and robustness. You will need to specify the request method (GET, POST, etc.), the URL of the API endpoint, and any necessary headers, including your API key. Handling the response is equally important, as the data returned by the API will typically need to be parsed and processed to fit your application's needs.

Error handling is a crucial aspect when integrating third-party APIs. Network issues, invalid API keys, or unexpected response formats can lead to errors that may disrupt your application. Implementing robust error handling routines will ensure your application can gracefully manage these issues without crashing. Logging errors and providing user-friendly messages will enhance the overall user experience and make troubleshooting easier.

Finally, consider the implications of integrating third-party APIs into your application. While they can provide significant benefits, such as reduced development time and access to advanced features, they also introduce dependencies that may affect your application's performance and reliability. It is vital to assess the stability and reputation of the API provider before integration. Regularly reviewing the API documentation for changes or updates will help you maintain compatibility and ensure your application continues to function smoothly. By understanding these principles, you can effectively integrate third-party APIs into your PHP applications, enhancing their capabilities and providing users with a richer experience.

Case Studies of Successful PHP Database Projects

In the realm of web development, PHP has emerged as a popular choice for building dynamic and data-driven applications. This subchapter examines several case studies of successful PHP database projects that illustrate the capabilities of PHP in managing and interacting with databases. These examples serve as practical learning experiences for beginners, showcasing how PHP can be harnessed to create efficient and robust applications.

One notable case study is an e-commerce platform developed for a small business. The project utilized PHP in conjunction with MySQL to create a user-friendly interface for customers and a powerful backend for inventory management. By implementing a relational database structure, the developers ensured that product information, customer data, and order histories were seamlessly connected. This allowed the business to track sales in real-time and manage stock levels effectively. The success of this project not only increased the client's revenue but also highlighted how PHP can facilitate complex data interactions in a straightforward manner.

Another inspiring example is a content management system (CMS) designed for a local non-profit organization. The PHP-based CMS enabled the organization to easily update their website content without needing extensive technical knowledge. Utilizing a MySQL database, the project allowed users to create, edit, and delete articles, manage event listings, and maintain a directory of resources. This case study illustrates how PHP can be used to empower non-technical users, making it an excellent choice for community-driven initiatives. The simplicity and flexibility of PHP, combined with the power of a database, resulted in a highly functional and user-friendly solution.

A third case study involves a social networking site built with PHP and PostgreSQL. This project focused on user engagement, allowing members to create profiles, connect with friends, and share content. The developers leveraged PHP to handle user authentication, profile management, and data retrieval from the PostgreSQL database. By utilizing advanced features such as indexing and relationships within the database, the application ensured quick access to user-generated content. The success of this social platform not only demonstrated the scalability of PHP applications but also highlighted best practices in database design and optimization.

Lastly, a project aimed at streamlining hotel management systems serves as an excellent example of PHP's capabilities in handling complex data structures. The system integrated various modules for booking management, customer relationship management, and reporting. By employing PHP alongside an SQLite database, the developers were able to create a lightweight yet powerful application that improved operational efficiency for the hotel. This case study showcases how PHP can adapt to different project scales and requirements, making it an invaluable tool for developers looking to implement database solutions across various industries.

These case studies collectively illustrate the versatility and effectiveness of PHP in developing database-driven applications. For beginners, they provide a clear understanding of how PHP can be applied to real-world scenarios, highlighting the importance of database management and the potential for career growth in the field of web development. As learners explore these examples, they can gain insights into best practices and innovative approaches that can inspire their own projects.

Chapter 11: Future Trends in PHP and Databases

Emerging Technologies in Web Development

Emerging technologies in web development are reshaping the landscape of how applications are built, deployed, and maintained. As the demand for dynamic and interactive web experiences grows, several technologies have gained prominence in the development community. Among these, Progressive Web Apps (PWAs) are becoming increasingly popular due to their ability to provide a native app-like experience directly in the browser. By leveraging the capabilities of modern web browsers, PWAs allow developers to create fast, reliable, and engaging applications that can work offline and send push notifications, thereby enhancing user engagement.

Another significant trend is the adoption of serverless architectures. This approach enables developers to build and run applications without having to manage server infrastructure. With serverless computing, developers can focus on writing code while cloud providers handle the scaling and management of servers. This model fosters rapid development and deployment, allowing web applications to respond to varying workloads without the need for continuous server maintenance. For beginners in PHP and databases, understanding how to integrate serverless functions with traditional database management can provide a solid foundation for modern web applications.

The rise of artificial intelligence and machine learning has also started to influence web development. These technologies are being utilized to create more personalized and adaptive user experiences. For example, AI-driven chatbots can enhance customer support on websites, while machine learning algorithms can analyze user behavior to provide tailored content and recommendations. For those learning PHP, incorporating AI tools can add significant value to web applications, making them more intelligent and responsive to user needs.

Additionally, the integration of APIs and microservices architecture is revolutionizing how web applications are structured. By breaking down applications into smaller, independent services, developers can improve scalability and maintainability. This modular approach allows teams to work on different components simultaneously, speeding up the development process. For students and career changers, understanding how to work with APIs and microservices can open doors to building complex applications that are easier to manage and evolve over time.

Finally, the increasing importance of responsive design cannot be overlooked. As users access the web from a variety of devices, ensuring that applications provide a seamless experience across desktops, tablets, and smartphones is crucial. Techniques such as flexible grid layouts, responsive images, and media queries are essential for achieving this goal. For beginners in PHP and databases, mastering responsive design principles can significantly enhance the usability and accessibility of web applications, ultimately leading to better user satisfaction and engagement.

The Role of Cloud Databases

Cloud databases have revolutionized the way data is stored and managed, offering significant advantages over traditional on-premises solutions. For career-changed professionals and students, understanding cloud databases is essential, especially in the context of PHP development. These databases provide flexibility, scalability, and accessibility, allowing users to manage their data from anywhere with an internet connection. This shift to the cloud enables developers to focus on application development without the burden of maintaining hardware or infrastructure.

One of the primary benefits of cloud databases is their scalability. As your application grows, so do your database needs. Cloud solutions allow you to easily scale up or down based on demand, ensuring that resources are allocated efficiently. For beginners in PHP development, this means you can start with a small database for a simple project and seamlessly expand it as your user base increases. This elasticity is particularly advantageous for those entering the tech field, as it removes the fear of over-investing in infrastructure that may become obsolete as projects evolve.

Another key aspect of cloud databases is their cost-effectiveness. Traditional database management systems often require significant upfront investments in hardware and software. In contrast, cloud databases typically operate on a pay-as-you-go model, allowing users to only pay for what they use. This is particularly appealing to students and professionals transitioning careers, as it lowers the barrier to entry for experimenting with database technologies. With minimal financial risk, learners can explore and implement various database solutions without the pressure of hefty initial costs.

Moreover, cloud databases offer enhanced collaboration features. With traditional databases, sharing data across teams can be cumbersome and time-consuming. Cloud solutions allow multiple users to access and modify the database concurrently, making it easier for teams to work together in real-time. For those new to PHP and database management, this collaborative environment fosters learning and innovation, as individuals can share insights and solutions more freely. It also aligns with modern development practices, where agile methodologies and teamwork are paramount.

Finally, security and disaster recovery are critical components of cloud databases. Leading cloud service providers invest heavily in security measures, including data encryption, access controls, and regular backups. This level of protection can be daunting for beginners to implement on their own with traditional databases. By leveraging cloud databases, users can benefit from these advanced security features without needing extensive expertise. Understanding these elements is crucial for new learners, as it ensures that they can build applications that are not only functional but also secure and resilient against potential data loss.

Continuous Learning and Resources

Continuous learning is essential for anyone venturing into the world of PHP databases, especially for career-changed professionals and students who may be new to programming. The technology landscape is ever-evolving, and staying updated with the latest advancements, trends, and best practices is crucial. Engaging in continuous learning helps individuals build a strong foundational knowledge while also allowing them to adapt to new challenges in the field. This commitment to growth not only enhances professional skills but also boosts confidence when tackling real-world projects.

One effective way to facilitate continuous learning is through online courses and tutorials specifically designed for PHP and database management. Numerous educational platforms offer structured programs that cater to beginners, often including video lectures, hands-on exercises, and assessments to reinforce learning. These resources allow learners to progress at their own pace, making it easier for those balancing other commitments to fit education into their schedules. Additionally, many courses provide a community forum where students can ask questions and share insights, fostering a collaborative learning environment.

In addition to structured courses, documentation and official resources play a vital role in ongoing education. The PHP manual and database documentation, such as that for MySQL, are invaluable references that provide detailed information on syntax, functions, and best practices. Familiarizing oneself with these resources not only helps in resolving specific coding issues but also encourages a deeper understanding of the language and its capabilities. Regularly consulting documentation can lead to discovering new functionalities and techniques that enhance programming skills and efficiency.

Participating in community forums and user groups can further enrich the learning experience. Platforms like Stack Overflow, Reddit, and dedicated PHP forums allow individuals to engage with other learners and experienced developers. By asking questions, sharing knowledge, and collaborating on projects, learners can gain diverse perspectives and insights that are often not available in traditional learning environments. Networking with others in the field can also lead to mentorship opportunities and collaborations that can enhance professional growth.

Lastly, practicing coding through real-life projects is one of the most effective methods for solidifying knowledge. By applying what has been learned in practical scenarios, individuals can improve their problem-solving abilities and gain hands-on experience with PHP databases. Whether it's building a personal project, contributing to open-source software, or working on freelance assignments, these experiences can significantly boost a learner's confidence and capability. Continuous learning is not just about consuming information; it is about actively engaging with the material and applying it in meaningful ways.

Chapter 12: Conclusion and Next Steps

Recap of Key Concepts

In this section, we will recap the key concepts covered throughout the book to reinforce your understanding of PHP and database integration. We began by introducing the importance of PHP as a server-side scripting language, particularly in the context of web development. PHP's ability to interact with databases is crucial for creating dynamic web applications, and understanding this interaction lays the foundation for developing robust applications. We explored how PHP can communicate with various database management systems, with a focus on MySQL as the most commonly used relational database.

Next, we delved into the fundamentals of database design and structure. This included an overview of tables, records, and fields, which are the building blocks of any database. A well-structured database is essential for efficient data retrieval and manipulation. We emphasized the importance of normalization and how it helps to eliminate redundancy, ensuring that the database remains organized and efficient. Understanding these concepts is vital for anyone looking to work with PHP and databases effectively.

We also covered the PHP Data Objects (PDO) extension, a powerful way to interact with databases securely and efficiently. We highlighted the benefits of using PDO, such as its support for multiple database types and prepared statements, which help to prevent SQL injection attacks. Learning how to use PDO effectively equips learners with the necessary skills to write secure and maintainable code. This is particularly important for career changers who may encounter various security concerns in their new roles.

In addition to the technical aspects, we discussed best practices for error handling and debugging in PHP. Understanding how to manage errors gracefully is crucial for maintaining a positive user experience and ensuring that applications run smoothly. We provided strategies for logging errors and using try-catch blocks to manage exceptions, which are essential skills for both students and professionals transitioning into PHP development.

Finally, we touched upon the importance of continuous learning and staying updated with the latest trends in PHP and database management. The tech landscape is ever-evolving, and being adaptable will serve you well in your career. As you continue your journey in mastering PHP and databases, remember that the concepts and techniques discussed in this book are just the beginning. By building upon this foundation, you will be well-equipped to take on more complex projects and challenges in the future.

Building a Portfolio

Building a portfolio is a crucial step for anyone looking to establish a career in PHP databases, especially for career-changed professionals and students of all ages. A well-crafted portfolio not only showcases your skills but also reflects your understanding of PHP and database management concepts. It serves as a tangible demonstration of your abilities to potential employers or clients, setting you apart in a competitive job market. This chapter will guide you through the essential components of building an effective portfolio that highlights your journey and expertise in PHP databases.

The first step in building your portfolio is to gather and curate your best work. Start by selecting projects that demonstrate a variety of skills and knowledge in PHP and database management. Whether these projects are from coursework, personal endeavors, or freelance work, they should illustrate your proficiency in coding, database design, and problem-solving. Include a mix of small and large projects, showcasing different aspects of PHP, such as CRUD operations, authentication systems, and integration with various databases like MySQL or PostgreSQL. This diversity will give viewers a comprehensive view of your capabilities.

Next, it's essential to provide context for each project in your portfolio. For every piece of work you showcase, include a brief description that outlines the project's objectives, your role, the technologies used, and the outcomes achieved. This narrative not only offers insight into your thought process but also allows potential employers to understand how you approach challenges.

Highlight any specific problems you solved, innovations you introduced, or lessons learned throughout the project. This storytelling aspect can significantly enhance the impact of your portfolio.

Another important element to consider is the presentation of your portfolio. A clean, professional layout is key to making a good impression. Whether you choose to create a personal website or use a platform like GitHub or Behance, ensure that your portfolio is easy to navigate and visually appealing. Include sections for different types of projects, testimonials if available, and links to live demos or repositories. Visual aids such as screenshots or diagrams can also help illustrate your work effectively. Remember, the goal is to make your portfolio as user-friendly and engaging as possible.

Lastly, keep your portfolio updated as you continue to learn and grow in your PHP database journey. Regularly adding new projects, refining existing ones, and showcasing any additional skills or certifications will demonstrate your commitment to professional development. Engaging with the PHP community—through forums, social media, or local meetups—can also provide valuable feedback and inspire new project ideas. By maintaining a dynamic portfolio, you not only present your current capabilities but also reflect your evolving expertise, making you a more attractive candidate to employers in the ever-changing tech landscape.

Resources for Continued Learning

In the ever-evolving landscape of web development, continuous learning is essential, especially for professionals transitioning into new careers or students embarking on their educational journeys. For those delving into PHP databases, various resources are available to enhance understanding and skill development. Online platforms, such as Coursera, Udemy, and edX, offer structured courses designed for beginners, covering fundamental concepts of PHP and database management. These platforms provide flexibility, allowing learners to study at their own pace while accessing high-quality content from industry experts.

In addition to online courses, documentation and official manuals serve as valuable resources. The PHP manual is an extensive resource that includes comprehensive information about the language's functions, features, and best practices. It often contains practical examples and user-contributed notes, making it accessible for learners at all levels. For database management systems like MySQL, the official documentation provides insights into installation, configuration, and advanced features, crucial for understanding how to integrate PHP with databases effectively.

Books authored by industry professionals can also play a significant role in continued learning. Titles such as "PHP and MySQL Web Development" by Luke Welling and Laura Thomson offer in-depth coverage of both PHP and MySQL, with practical examples and exercises that reinforce learning. These books are designed to cater to beginners and can be excellent references for more advanced topics as one's skills progress. Additionally, eBooks and guides available through platforms like O'Reilly or Packt Publishing can provide a wealth of knowledge tailored to specific areas of interest within PHP and databases.

Engaging with online communities and forums can further enhance learning experiences. Websites like Stack Overflow, Reddit, and PHP-specific forums allow learners to ask questions, share insights, and seek advice from experienced developers. These interactions foster a sense of belonging and can provide practical solutions to common challenges faced while learning PHP and database integration. Networking in these communities can also lead to mentorship opportunities, offering beginners guidance from those who have successfully navigated similar career transitions.

Finally, hands-on practice is crucial for solidifying knowledge and gaining practical experience. Platforms like GitHub provide an opportunity to collaborate on open-source projects, allowing learners to apply their skills in real-world scenarios. Participating in coding challenges on sites like LeetCode or HackerRank can also sharpen problem-solving abilities and enhance understanding of PHP and database interactions.

By leveraging these resources, career-changed professionals and students can build a solid foundation in PHP databases, equipping themselves for success in their new ventures.

Understanding API's

Understanding APIs is crucial for anyone venturing into the realm of web development, particularly when working with PHP and databases. An Application Programming Interface (API) acts as a bridge between different software applications, allowing them to communicate and interact with one another. In the context of PHP databases, APIs enable developers to perform operations such as retrieving, updating, and deleting data without needing to understand the complexities of the underlying database structure. This abstraction simplifies the development process, making it accessible for beginners who may not have a deep technical background.

APIs can be categorized into various types, including RESTful APIs and SOAP APIs, each with its own set of rules and conventions. RESTful APIs, which are more commonly used in contemporary web applications, rely on standard HTTP methods such as GET, POST, PUT, and DELETE to perform operations on resources. This stateless architecture allows for scalability and flexibility, making it ideal for applications that require real-time data access.

For new learners, understanding these methods is essential, as they form the backbone of how data is exchanged between a PHP application and a database.

When working with PHP, developers can easily integrate APIs into their applications using built-in functions and libraries. The cURL library, for example, is a powerful tool that allows PHP scripts to communicate with other servers via APIs. By sending HTTP requests and handling responses, developers can interact with databases hosted on remote servers. This capability opens up numerous possibilities for creating dynamic applications that can fetch real-time data from various sources, enhancing the user experience without the need for complex coding.

Security is another critical aspect to consider when working with APIs. As data is transferred between the client and server, it is vital to implement authentication and authorization mechanisms to protect sensitive information. Common methods include using API keys and OAuth tokens to verify user identities and permissions. For those new to programming, grasping the importance of security measures is essential, as it helps prevent data breaches and ensures that only authorized users can access specific resources.

In summary, understanding APIs is foundational for anyone looking to build PHP applications that interact with databases. The ability to communicate with other systems through APIs opens up a world of possibilities for developers, allowing them to create robust, scalable, and secure applications. By mastering the principles of APIs, beginners can enhance their skill set and significantly improve their employability in the tech job market. This knowledge prepares learners for future advancements in web technology.

Hotkeys and Commands in Development Environments

General (Works Across Languages)

- **Code Comments:**
  - Single line:
    - `Ctrl + /` or `Cmd + /`
  - Multi-line:
    - `Shift + Alt + A` (Visual Studio Code)
- **Auto-format Code:**
  - `Shift + Alt + F` or `Shift + Cmd + F` (Visual Studio Code)
- **Run Code:**
  - PHP: `php <filename>.php`
  - Java: `javac <filename>.java` followed by `java <classname>`
  - Node.js: `node <filename>.js`
- **Open Integrated Terminal:**
  - ``Ctrl + ` `` or ``Cmd + ` `` (backtick)

PHP: Common Commands and Snippets

1. **Basic Syntax for Starting a Script:**

```
php
Copy code
<?php
echo "Hello, World!";
?>
```

2. **Create an Associative Array:**

```
php
Copy code
$user = [
    "name" => "Alice",
    "age" => 25
];
echo $user["name"]; // Output: Alice
```

3. **Connect to a MySQL Database:**

```
php
Copy code
$conn = new mysqli("localhost",
"username", "password", "database");
if ($conn->connect_error) {
    die("Connection failed: " . $conn-
>connect_error);
}
echo "Connected successfully";
```

4. **Hotkeys in PHP Development (Visual Studio Code):**
    - **Auto-close tags:** Enabled by default in PHP extensions.
    - **Duplicate Line:** `Shift + Alt + Down Arrow`

www.ingramcontent.com/pod-product-compliance
Lightning Source LLC
LaVergne TN
LVHW082356200926
848481LV00012B/3580

* 9 7 9 8 3 4 9 4 4 9 1 2 3 *